MATHEMATICS THEIR WAY®
BEYOND THE BOOK

ACTIVITIES and PROJECTS

from

CLASSROOMS LIKE YOURS

MATHEMATICS THEIR WAY®
BEYOND THE BOOK

ACTIVITIES and PROJECTS

from

CLASSROOMS LIKE YOURS

Center for Innovation in Education

Addison-Wesley

Addison Wesley Longman, Inc.

Menlo Park, California • Reading, Massachusetts • New York • Don Mills, Ontario • Wokingham, England
Amsterdam • Bonn • Sydney • Singapore • Tokyo • Madrid • San Juan • Paris • Seoul • Milan • Mexico City • Taipei, Taiwan

This book is published by Addison-Wesley, an imprint of Addison Wesley Longman, Inc.

Editorial Director: Patricia Brill
Managing Editor: Catherine Anderson
Project Editor: Jeri Hayes
Design Manager: Jeff Kelly
Production Director: Janet Yearian
Production Coordinator: Shannon Miller
Production: David Forrest, Laurel Patton, David Woods
Text and Cover Design: Remen-Willis Design Group
Photography: Scott Campbell

ISBN 0-201-49334-9
1 2 3 4 5 6 7 8 9 10–BAM–00 99 98 97 96

CONTENTS

INTRODUCTION

Mathematics Their Way® is more than a mathematics program for the primary grades—it is a way of teaching children mathematics built on ideas developed by Mary Baratta-Lorton while she was teaching in the primary grades. Because of her philosophy of looking to the children for ways of teaching that would work, she was open to learning from the children how to teach mathematics their way. She shared many of her ways of teaching with other teachers who, in turn, encouraged her to write down her ideas. Those ideas became the book **Mathematics Their Way**. First published more than twenty years ago, this teacher resource book has had a tremendous impact on the way that mathematics is taught in the primary grades. It continues to be widely used today in classrooms across the country even though no revision of the original book has ever been made.

This book is dedicated to all the **Mathematics Their Way** teachers who have guided and helped millions of primary school children to appreciate and experience mathematics their way. Some of these teachers may themselves have learned mathematics as children in **Mathematics Their Way** classrooms. Many of these teachers have gone beyond the book, building on it and what they have learned from the children in their classes, to teach mathematics their own way. They have built on the ideas of **Mathematics Their Way** and extended the activities to make learning mathematics even more engaging, more enjoyable, and more effective for the children in their classrooms.

Over the years, many teachers have shared their new ways of thinking about teaching mathematics both with us as publishers and with the Center for Innovation in Education. At the time of her death, Mary Baratta-Lorton was Director of Early Childhood Education at the Center, which she had founded with her husband, Bob. The Center is a nonprofit educational institution established to develop, evaluate, and further the use of successful innovative methods and materials in elementary school education. Teachers have told us about the variety of ways they have extended activities and sent us the results of many projects that the children in their classrooms have done.

Because of the many inspiring ideas we have seen, we thought that such ideas could be brought together in a book that would serve as a catalyst for **Mathematics Their Way** teachers. So we worked with the Center for Innovation in Education to extend an invitation to teachers everywhere to send in examples of student work on activities and projects that went beyond the ideas in **Mathematics Their Way**. We especially wanted to see activities and projects that connected mathematics with the special interests of the children in a classroom, perhaps through an unusual theme, a different curriculum area, or a special seasonal celebration.

Teachers from all over the world as well as from all parts of the United States sent in wonderful examples of the work that their students were doing. Many of the activities were motivated by suggestions from children while the class was doing **Mathematics Their Way** activities or during other times of the school day, when they saw a new way to connect what they were learning or doing with mathematics. We received graphs, charts, photos, slides, constructions, mobiles, and all sorts of artwork. Teachers told us about activities that built on all of the mathematical strands of **Mathematics Their Way**; that were done by students in all the grades from kindergarten through fourth; and that came from all kinds of classroom situations, including mixed grades, special education classes, and multilingual classes.

Reviewing the submissions was both enjoyable and satisfying, because we knew that the creativity and care in teaching shown by these contributions was supported by the book that Addison-Wesley Innovative first published in 1975. It was, however, very difficult to choose which pieces would appear in this book. Finally, we selected the twenty-eight that you see in this book, not because they were better than the others, but because they truly represent the many innovative and interesting ideas embedded in all the submissions. We want to thank all the teachers who took the time to send us so many splendid examples of creative activities and good mathematics teaching from their classrooms.

The pages that follow are both a sharing and a celebrating of children doing and enjoying mathematics in a variety of settings. Each activity is referenced to the **Mathematics Their Way** chapter on which it was built. The teacher's name, grade level, and school are listed, along with the concepts, connections, and materials associated with the activity. We have also provided the teacher's short description of what the children did. These descriptions are not offered as instructions for you to carry out the activity in your classroom, although you could do any of them with the given information. Rather we want to inspire you too to build on the **Mathematics Their Way** foundation and find ways to connect mathematics to the unique interests of the children in your classroom.

Many of the activities are not especially uncommon; most are adaptations of timeless, classic classroom activities. Good teachers everywhere see or hear about an activity, and they take it, adapt it, and make it their own. We hope that by sharing the creativity of these activities with you, you and the children in your classroom will create the next generation of ideas to be shared with others. Please let us hear from you.

The Publisher

Bilingual Homework

What kind of homework do you like doing with your child?

¿Que tipo de tarea le gusta hacer con su hijo o hija?

hacer algo

Graphing

▼

Teachers
Melissa Bornstein and Linda Loughrin
First and Second Grades

School
Bijou Elementary School
South Lake Tahoe, California

Concepts
Organizing data, graphing

Connections
Parents' night theme

Materials
Poster board, survey sheets, marking pens

This activity was started on the day of the first Parents' Night (three weeks after the start of school). During class the children completed surveys telling what kind of homework they preferred to have. We made a graph of the class data and discussed our results. That evening parents were asked to complete the same survey before they saw the results of the children's preferences. It was fun to watch parents comparing their responses with those of the children. In class the next day, the children compared the results of the two surveys. For this activity, results for both children and parents were compared for English-speaking and Spanish-speaking groups.

Mobiles

Teacher
Carla Farren, Kindergarten

School
Mater Dolorosa School
South San Francisco, California

Concepts
Patterns, symmetry

Connections
Art

Materials
Construction paper in different colors cut in circles and in pattern block shapes, hole punch, fishing line

The children folded their circles in quarters to locate the center and glued a hexagon shape in the center. Then using other shapes one shape at a time, they placed and glued shapes point to point or side to side on the hexagon and went all the way around the circle. They continued with different shapes until the circle was covered with shapes. Each child made two circles and then glued them, back to back. Then we punched holes in them, strung them with fishing line, and hung them in the room.

Counting

▼

MATHEMATICS THEIR WAY
Chapter 4

Teacher
Deborah Nichols, First Grade

School
Rollinsford Grade School
Rollinsford, New Hampshire

Concepts
Counting, tallying, probability

Connections
Social studies, Presidents' Day theme

Materials
100 grid (large enough for coin stamps to fit in squares), coin stamps, stamp pads, real coins, tally sheets

We carried out this experiment as part of our Presidents' Day math activity. The children worked in groups of three, with three jobs: coin tosser, stamper, and tallier. When the coin was tossed, the stamper recorded the result on the 100 grid, and the tallier made a mark on the tally sheet. Each group recorded the results of 100 coin tosses, tallied the results, and compared their results with those of other groups. All children respected their roles and were actively involved in the work. A lot of counting followed this activity as the children checked and rechecked their work.

In one group, the children decided on their own to use different ink colors to identify heads and tails so that they could do the counting/checking more easily and quickly.

The cooperative efforts were tremendous. Involvement was high and intense while the noise level was low. As extras, the children learned to identify coins and to recognize heads and tails. All the work was displayed on a bulletin board, and the children spent much time analyzing the results.

Presidents' Day

Coin Toss

B

5¢ + 49 = 10

Heads	Tails
卅卅 ‖‖‖ 卅卅 卅卅 卅卅 卅卅 卅卅 卅卅	‖ 卅卅 卅卅 卅卅 卅卅 卅卅 卅卅 卅卅 ‖‖‖

F

15 53 47

Counting with Turkeys

Teacher
Kathy Thompson, Second Grade

School
Nevis School
Nevis, Minnesota

Concepts
Counting

Connections
Thanksgiving theme, art

Materials
Butcher paper, brown construction paper (1-2 sheets per student), paints, crayons, markers, scraps of colored paper, scissors

The children traced and cut around their hands on brown construction paper. They glued the "turkey hands" onto a long piece of butcher paper. Then we wrote the numbers by 5s under each hand of 5 fingers. Afterwards the children added details to the background.

This is a great activity both for teaching and reinforcing the concept of counting by 5s around Thanksgiving time!

Pop-Up Number Book

Counting
▼

MATHEMATICS THEIR WAY
Chapter 4

Teacher
Loreli E. Stochaj, First Grade

School
Franklin School
Summit, New Jersey

Concepts
Counting, number sense

Connections
Art

Materials
10 large sheets of butcher or poster paper, twine or yarn

We were so busy discussing numbers that the students began to notice them in everyday life. We labeled big sheets of paper with the numerals from 0 to 9 on the sheets (one number per sheet) and made a big book using yarn to hold the sheets together. Whenever someone thought of something that came in groups of a certain number, we would record it on that sheet. For example, 5 fingers or 5 points on a star went on the 5 sheet.

The best thing about this activity is that the students initiated it and looked everyday, in and out of school, for ways to add to the book. The parents thought it was great fun, too!

fingers

senses

players on one team on basketball

five

nickel

fan blades

school days

toe nails

finger nails

toes

Starfish legs

quintuplets

points on a Sta⭐

5 to

quintuplets

5, 10, 15, 20, 25...

shoes

1+1

5-3

6, 18...

Immigration Pictograph

Pictograph of 4th Grade Ethnic Bac

Completed by Mrs. Saunders

Ireland	
Italy	
Germany	
Holland	
China	
Scotland	
Mexico	
Spain	
Puerto Rico	

Graphing

▼

MATHEMATICS THEIR WAY
Chapter 6

Teacher
Joanne Hines Saunders, Fourth Grade

School
Little Britain Elementary School
Newburgh, New York

Concepts
Graphing, problem solving

Connections
Social studies: immigration in America

Materials
Construction paper, glue

As part of our study of New York State history, our fourth-grade class did intensive research on Ellis Island and the effects of immigration on New York State history. In conjunction with this, each student researched his or her ethnic background and family tree to write autobiographies. A "Great American Fest" was the culmination of this unit.

We used this pictograph activity as a tool to launch group research about the children's individual backgrounds. The students decided on the manner of representation, such as shown in the key, because they knew that a pictograph uses pictures to show information and that each picture stands for a number of items.

After gathering data and constructing the pictograph, students were able to write various problem-solving questions, such as comparing the number of immigrants from one area to another, finding the number of responses, and so on. The pictograph allowed students to visualize their responses in a concrete way.

Teacher
Alice Reidl, Kindergarten

School
Tohajiilee Community School
Laguna, New Mexico

Concepts
Patterns

Connections
Special education, art, social studies: Native American studies

Materials
Colored felt squares (one per child), assorted scraps of colored felt, scissors, white glue, paper punch, yarn for fringe

We made these blankets during Native American Week at our all-Navajo school. We used blankets because many of the children see elders weaving blankets at home. The student who made this design has cerebral palsy, so this was a very successful project for him. We discussed patterns in weaving, and then the children set to work. We precut the shapes out of felt and used white glue to "stitch" them on the felt squares. Finally, we punched holes on both sides and used yarn for fringe.

Native American Blankets

Pumpkin Mobile

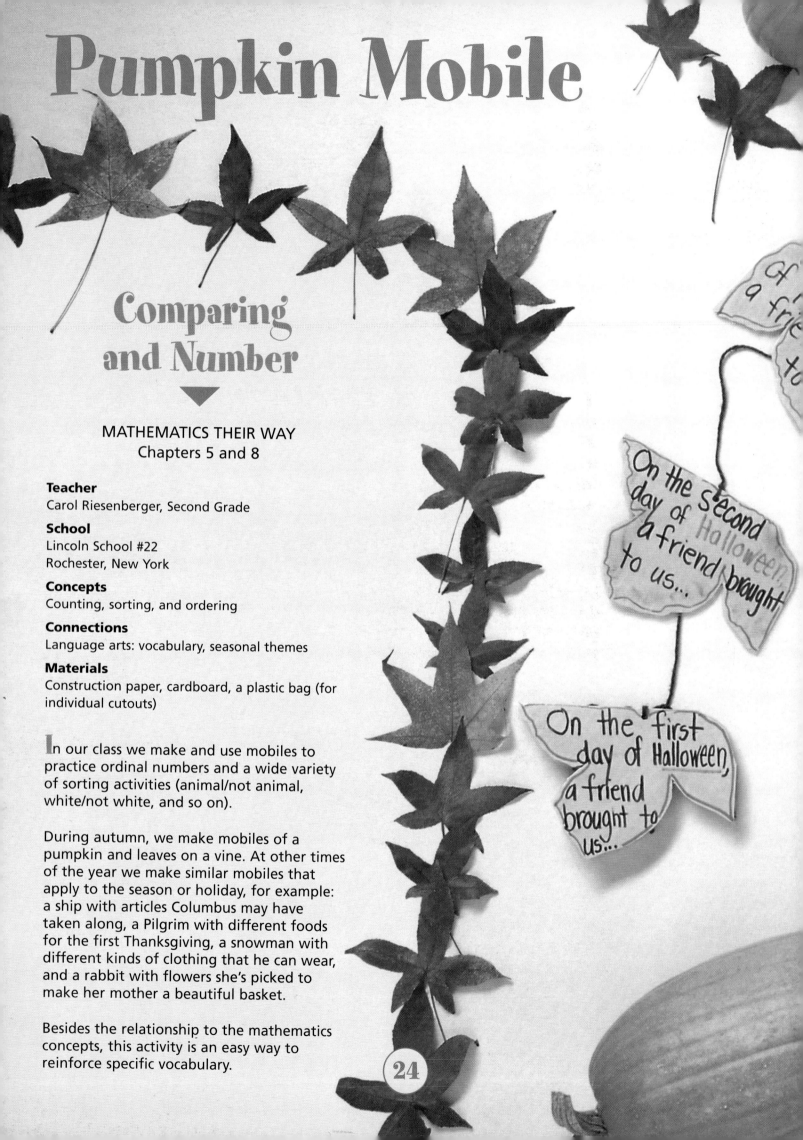

Comparing and Number

▼

MATHEMATICS THEIR WAY
Chapters 5 and 8

Teacher
Carol Riesenberger, Second Grade

School
Lincoln School #22
Rochester, New York

Concepts
Counting, sorting, and ordering

Connections
Language arts: vocabulary, seasonal themes

Materials
Construction paper, cardboard, a plastic bag (for individual cutouts)

In our class we make and use mobiles to practice ordinal numbers and a wide variety of sorting activities (animal/not animal, white/not white, and so on).

During autumn, we make mobiles of a pumpkin and leaves on a vine. At other times of the year we make similar mobiles that apply to the season or holiday, for example: a ship with articles Columbus may have taken along, a Pilgrim with different foods for the first Thanksgiving, a snowman with different kinds of clothing that he can wear, and a rabbit with flowers she's picked to make her mother a beautiful basket.

Besides the relationship to the mathematics concepts, this activity is an easy way to reinforce specific vocabulary.

On the second day of Halloween a friend brought to us...

On the first day of Halloween, a friend brought to us...

On the fourth day of Halloween, a friend brought to us...

third day

On the fifth day of Halloween a friend brought to us...

On the sixth day of Halloween a friend brought to us...

On the seventh day of Halloween a friend brought to us...

Chocolate Day

By: Brette Simmons and Kelly Roxn

W cho

We (26) sorted the

roups:

Chocolate Day

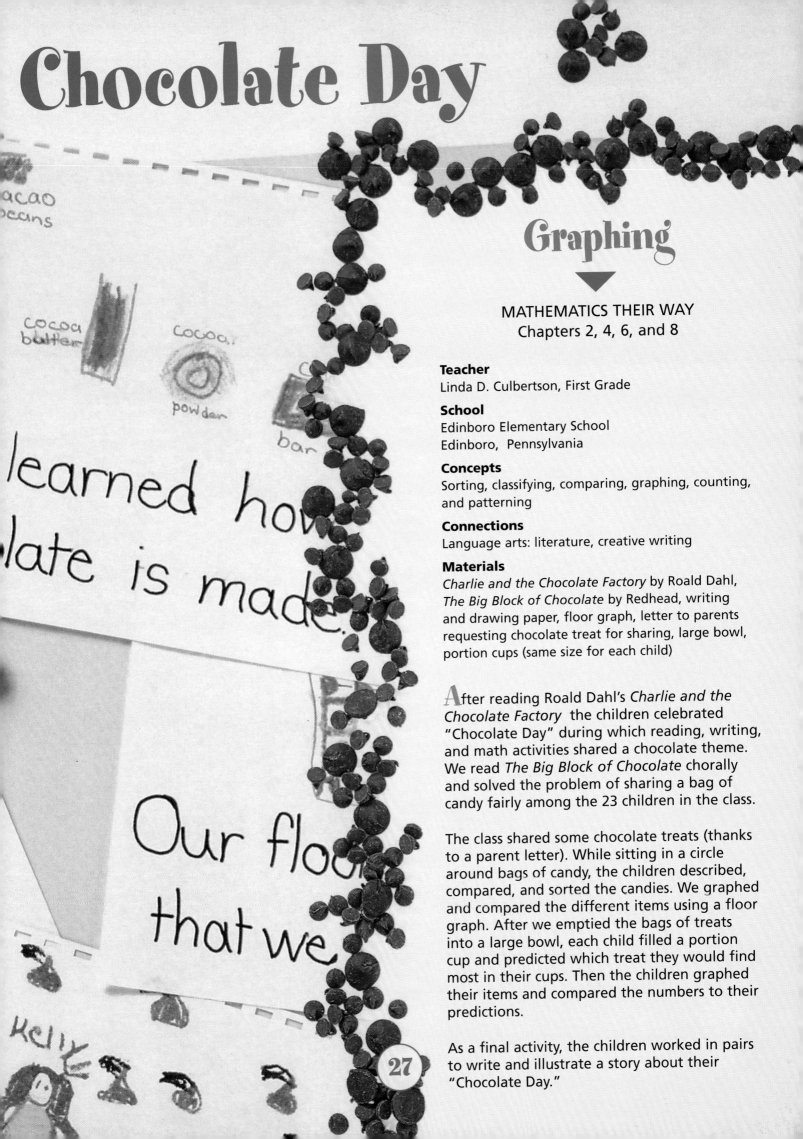

cacao beans

cocoa butter

cocoa powder

bar

learned how ... late is made.

Our floo ... that we

Kelly

Graphing

▼

MATHEMATICS THEIR WAY
Chapters 2, 4, 6, and 8

Teacher
Linda D. Culbertson, First Grade

School
Edinboro Elementary School
Edinboro, Pennsylvania

Concepts
Sorting, classifying, comparing, graphing, counting, and patterning

Connections
Language arts: literature, creative writing

Materials
Charlie and the Chocolate Factory by Roald Dahl, *The Big Block of Chocolate* by Redhead, writing and drawing paper, floor graph, letter to parents requesting chocolate treat for sharing, large bowl, portion cups (same size for each child)

After reading Roald Dahl's *Charlie and the Chocolate Factory* the children celebrated "Chocolate Day" during which reading, writing, and math activities shared a chocolate theme. We read *The Big Block of Chocolate* chorally and solved the problem of sharing a bag of candy fairly among the 23 children in the class.

The class shared some chocolate treats (thanks to a parent letter). While sitting in a circle around bags of candy, the children described, compared, and sorted the candies. We graphed and compared the different items using a floor graph. After we emptied the bags of treats into a large bowl, each child filled a portion cup and predicted which treat they would find most in their cups. Then the children graphed their items and compared the numbers to their predictions.

As a final activity, the children worked in pairs to write and illustrate a story about their "Chocolate Day."

Pattern Book Experiments

▼

MATHEMATICS THEIR WAY
Chapter 12

Teacher
Mary Ellen Collins, First and Second Grades

School
Elmwood School
Elmwood Park, Illinois

Concepts
Counting, counting money

Connections
Writing, real life: shopping

Materials
Construction paper, mailing tape

Because there is no teacher's aide in our class, when children practice money counting skills with each other, there is no way to be sure that they are coming up with the correct amount unless I am actively involved in the process. By making these wallets with various amounts of money taped inside, the answers can easily be checked. The children were able to practice money counting independently. They also started to write story problems about the wallets. They loved to see their names on the wallets and to hear story problems written about them.

Choose a Wallet

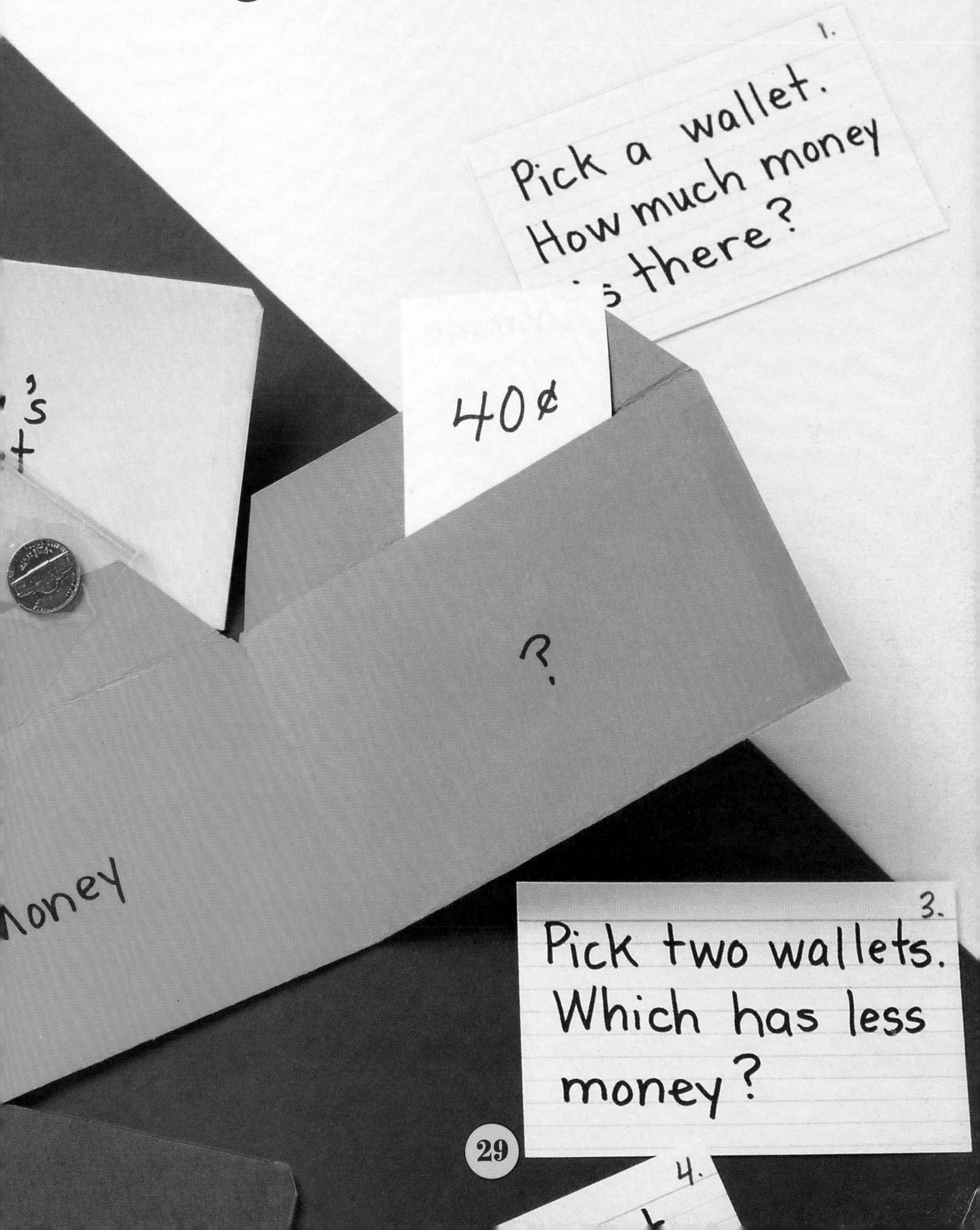

1.

Pick a wallet.
How much money
is there?

40¢

's
t

?

money

3.

Pick two wallets.
Which has less
money?

4.

Our Pets
3H PET GRAPH

Information We Gathered From Our Gra[ph]

1. We have 18 different kinds of pets
2. More _people_ have cats (7 people) than any other
3. 4 people own a total of 31 fish
4. 2 people own 92 chickens
5. 1 person (Nic) has 10,000 bees
6. 10 different categories of pets have only 1 person hav[e]
7. Nic has 9 different kinds of animals
8. Nicole has 5 different kinds of animals
9. We have 9½ class horses. The ½ is because one of

Animals →	Dogs	Cats	Gerbils	Pigs	Geese	Ants	Class Hamsters	Rabbits	Guinea p[ig]
Total →	8	15	1	2	2	.	1	1	2

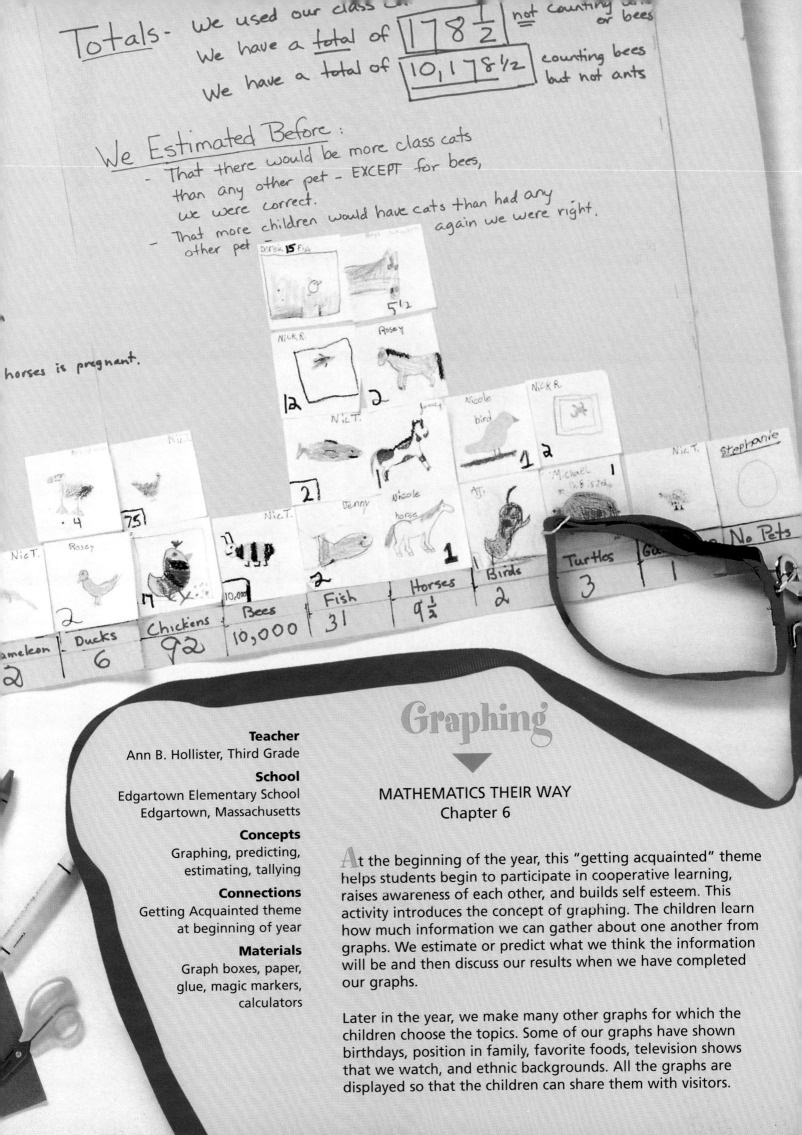

Totals- We used our class ca[...]
We have a total of | 178½ | = not counting a[...] or bees
We have a total of | 10,178½ | counting bees but not ants

We Estimated Before:
- That there would be more class cats than any other pet - EXCEPT for bees, we were correct.
- That more children would have cats than had any other pet _____ again we were right.

horses is pregnant.

Derek 15 Fish

5½

NICK R.   Rosey
12   2

NicT.
2

Nicole
bird
1   2

NICK R.

NicT.   Stephanie

Michael   1

No Pets

Jenny   Nicole
horse
2   1

A.J.

NicT.
Rosey
2

17   10,000

Birds   Turtles   Gu[...]
2   3   1

Chameleon   Ducks   Chickens   Bees   Fish   Horses
2   6   92   10,000   31   9½
.4   75

Graphing

Teacher
Ann B. Hollister, Third Grade

School
Edgartown Elementary School
Edgartown, Massachusetts

Concepts
Graphing, predicting, estimating, tallying

Connections
Getting Acquainted theme at beginning of year

Materials
Graph boxes, paper, glue, magic markers, calculators

MATHEMATICS THEIR WAY
Chapter 6

At the beginning of the year, this "getting acquainted" theme helps students begin to participate in cooperative learning, raises awareness of each other, and builds self esteem. This activity introduces the concept of graphing. The children learn how much information we can gather about one another from graphs. We estimate or predict what we think the information will be and then discuss our results when we have completed our graphs.

Later in the year, we make many other graphs for which the children choose the topics. Some of our graphs have shown birthdays, position in family, favorite foods, television shows that we watch, and ethnic backgrounds. All the graphs are displayed so that the children can share them with visitors.

Comparing

▼

MATHEMATICS THEIR WAY
Chapter 5

Teacher
Joanne Wills Minke, Kindergarten

School
Shorecrest Preparatory School
St. Petersburg, Florida

Concepts
Comparing, sorting

Connections
Social studies, language arts

Materials
2″ squares of construction paper, colored markers,
crayons

The children drew pictures of their houses
on squares of construction paper. They told
the class the names of their streets. The class
discussed the idea that there are different
kinds of streets that are called by different
names, such as: Avenue, Boulevard, Circle,
Court, Lane, Drive, Way, Street, and Highway.

The children who live on streets that have
the same kind of name grouped themselves
together. We then compared the sizes of
these groups, using the words *more*, *less*, and
the same. The children glued the squares
with their house pictures onto a graph
according to the names of the streets on
which they lived.

Names of Streets

Graphing

▼

MATHEMATICS THEIR WAY
Chapter 6

Teacher
Esther Abdel-Hameed, Kindergarten

School
American School of Kuwait
Hawalli, Kuwait

Concepts
Graphing, sorting and classifying

Connections
Social studies

Materials
Chart paper, "person" template, markers, crayons, scissors

At our school, children come from many different countries. While studying our unit on Kuwait, we discussed the various places we come from. We labeled the graph "Our Nationalities." Afterwards, we sorted or "patterned" children according to nationalities. We learn where we are from as we learned how to interpret the graph. And as a bonus, we learned to recognize each other's flags.

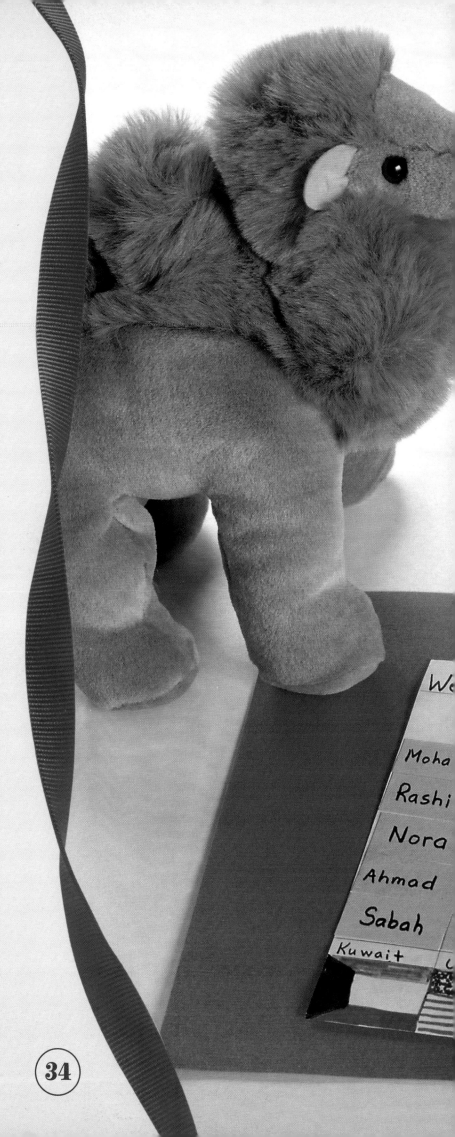

Our Nationalities

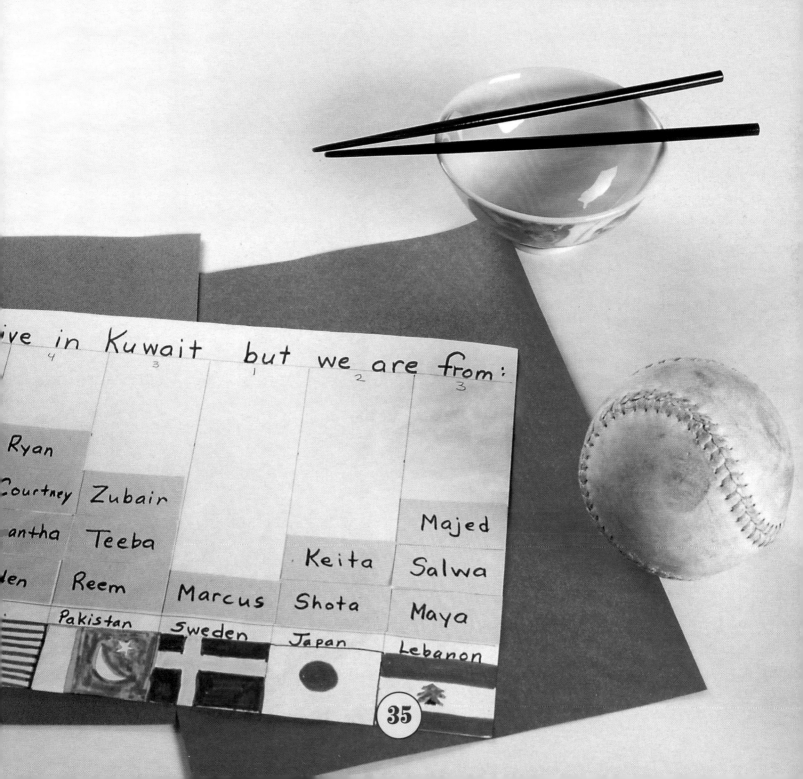

...ive in Kuwait but we are from:

4	3	1	2	3
Ryan				
Courtney	Zubair			
...antha	Teeba			Majed
			Keita	Salwa
...den	Reem	Marcus	Shota	Maya
Pakistan		Sweden	Japan	Lebanon

Our Beautiful Buttons

Our Beautiful Buttons

A.M. Kindergarten 1993

...day we coun...

...ay we cou...

On Wednesday we...

36

17 buttons.

35 buttons.

unted 33 buttons.

Counting

MATHEMATICS THEIR WAY
Chapter 4

Teacher
Janet Kulbiski, Kindergarten

School
Marlatt School
Manhattan, Kansas

Concepts
Counting

Connections
Language arts: alphabet

Materials
Unifix cubes, scissors, glue, assorted colors of construction paper, 5 white sheets of 12" x 18" construction paper, twine or yarn

In our language arts program we use the "letter people." Mr. B has beautiful buttons, so we decided to count our buttons.

Each child counted Unifix cubes to match the number of buttons she or he had that day. We snapped the Unifix cubes together into one long train and counted them. To record the number of buttons, we cut paper buttons from colored construction paper. We put a Unifix cube on each paper button as it was glued onto the page. When all the Unifix cubes were used, we knew that we had recorded all the buttons.

Mitten Math

Number
▼

MATHEMATICS THEIR WAY
Chapters 7, 8, and 9

Teacher
Bobbie Williams, Kindergarten

School
Brookwood Elementary School
Snellville, Georgia

Concepts
Counting, number sentences

Connections
Language arts

Materials
The Mitten by Jan Brett, sleeping bag, animal headbands, colored construction paper, yarn

We read *The Mitten* together. Then we retold the story to make a number story. The children acted out the story, using the sleeping bag as the mitten. As we came to situations with number sentences, I would model them for the children.

The children made paper mittens that they sewed together with yarn. Then they made paper animals and worked together in small groups to tell their own number stories. They made recordings and took them to the computer lab to write their own number stories.

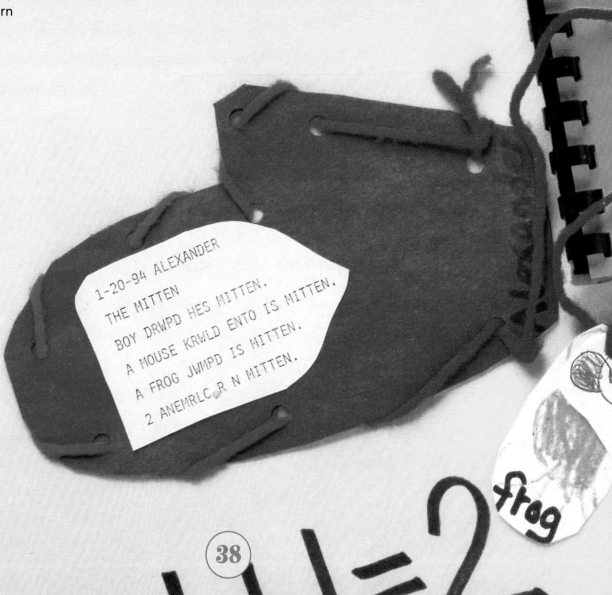

1-20-94 ALEXANDER
THE MITTEN
BOY DRWPD HES MITTEN.
A MOUSE KRWLD ENTO IS MITTEN.
A FROG JWMPD IS MITTEN.
2 ANEMRLC∞R N MITTEN.

frog

1 + 1 = 2

STEPHANIE

1-26-94   STEPHANIE
I   WUS   IN   THE   WOODS,
AND   I   LRSD.   A   MITTEN.   THE
BOD   WAT   IN
AND   THE   MOUSE   WAT   IN
AND   THE   CRICKET   AND   THE   BEAR
AND   THE   WOIF   WAT   IN
AND   THE   FOX   WAT   IN   THE
MITTEN.

Stephanie

$$1+1+1+1+1+1=6$$

Farm Or Zoo?

Graphing with our pictures... Favorite farm animals

EdM 294A
Patricia K.
Susami

Farm Animal Unit

Sorting Farm / Zoo Animals

Sorting and Classifying

▼

MATHEMATICS THEIR WAY
Chapter 3

Teacher
Patricia K. Susami, Special Education

School
Ben Franklin School
Menomonee Falls, Wisconsin

Concepts
Sorting, comparing, classifying

Connections
Science

Materials
Pictures cut from magazines of animals found in zoos and on farms, chart paper

My class is composed of six cognitively disabled children between the ages of 6 and 8. The children are included in nonacademic classes within the school and come to me for their academic subjects. My challenge has been to adapt *Mathematics Their Way* materials and methods to their ability levels.

I use many real models for the children, as they are basically at the concrete level. In the sorting activity, the children separate farm animals and zoo animals. This activity is difficult for some of them, especially since our local zoo contains a farm area.

At another time during this activity, the children place their pictures under the column headings of the animals they prefer. This helps the children begin to understand charts and to read in columns. The children then compare the numbers of animals, telling which group has more or less. Again this work is difficult for some of the children.

Sunnyside Up Or Down?

Graphing

▼

MATHEMATICS THEIR WAY
Chapter 6

Teacher
Carla Farren, Kindergarten

School
Mater Dolorosa School
South San Francisco, California

Concepts
Graphing, comparing

Connections
Health

Materials
Chart paper—one large sheet for the class, small sheets of paper—one per child

As the class brainstormed different ways that eggs can be cooked, we wrote each idea on the butcher paper. Next, each child drew an egg on a small sheet of paper. As the children took turns telling their favorite way to eat an egg, they put their eggs in the appropriate row on the chart. Then we discussed what way of cooking eggs was the most favorite in the class, the least favorite, the most unusual, and so on.

Fried   Scrambled   Boiled

Deviled Egg

Stuffed Eggs

Egg Sandwich

Poached

ny Side Up

H

Patterns

▼

Mathematics Their Way

Chapters 2 and 10

Teacher
Kathie Johnson, First and Second Grades

School
Shawnee Elementary School
West Chester, Ohio

Concepts
Using patterns, using grids

Connections
Social studies: American folk art forms

Materials
Unifix cubes, 10 different kinds of wrapping paper cut into 1" squares, 5" x 5" squares of construction paper, white glue, large sheet of paper (for mounting squares). (Hint: Seasonal gift wrap can be used to tie in with a holiday or season.)

For this pattern activity, each child worked to discover the pattern made up by the letters of his or her name on various sizes of grids. The children then constructed their names with Unifix cubes, attributing a different color Unifix cube to each different letter of their name. Each child snapped together a long train of his or her name pattern and compared it with a neighbor's train.

On another day, the children selected squares of gift wrap to translate the letter patterns of their names. First, they chose a different kind of gift wrap for each different letter in their names and then glued down their name pattern on a strip of paper. Then they sorted and compared the name strips. Using their name strips as a guide, the children then repeated their name pattern with gift wrap squares until they covered the 5" x 5" construction paper square. The quilt squares were placed into a class "I AM SPECIAL" quilt on a large sheet of paper.

Parents enjoyed this "quilt" at an open house while the children giggled at their parents' guesses about whose name each square represented. This was a wonderful culmination activity to a thematic unit on quilts. An appreciation for the art and mathematics involved in quilt making grew in the children. I believe they will continue to look at quilts and see them with more understanding eyes.

Friendship Quilt

Our Halloween Costumes

Wilcox F 11
Punahou School "Halloween Costume G

Madame Pele	Princesses	Knight	Ninjas	Happy Faced Spider	Pirates	Batman	S

Graphing

▼

MATHEMATICS THEIR WAY
Chapter 6

Teacher
Jonathan Yorck, Kindergarten

School
Punahou School

Honolulu, Hawaii

Concepts
Sorting, graphing

Connections
Halloween theme

Materials
Camera, film, poster board

Making graphs is an enjoyable activity in our class. At our school Halloween party, while taking pictures of the children in their costumes, we had the idea of graphing different kinds of costumes. Every year there is a high representation of princesses and pirates, but notice our Happy-Faced Spider and Madame Pele, the volcano goddess in Hawaii. Making this graph was great fun and an excellent learning experience!

Honolulu, Hawaii

Unicorn   Cheerleader

Patterns

Teacher
Libby Underhill, First Grade

School
Lincoln Elementary School
Bemidji, Minnesota

Concepts
Patterns

Connections
Science, nature

Materials
Instant camera, film, photo album

As an extension of the patterning concept emphasized in Chapter Two of *Mathematics Their Way*, my first graders take a "pattern walk." We search the neighborhood for patterns in the environment and record them with an instant camera. This is a great way to involve parents! On returning to the classroom, we compile the photographs in an album. As you can see by its worn features, it's a favorite of the class!

With this activity, the children learn that patterns are found everywhere and are a natural part of the environment. As one child responded, "It's what makes the world *beautiful!*"

Pattern Walk Photo Album

Cookie Math

The Cookie Cooling Sheet

Our group of 3 p
baked 12 cookies

37 38 39 40

42 43 44 45 46 47 48 49 50

52 53 54 55 56 57 58 59 60

62 63 64 65 66 67 68

baked (68) cookies.
have (22) children in our class fami
will each get 3 cookies. Mrs. Young can
that are left o

Counting and Place Value

MATHEMATICS THEIR WAY
Chapters 4 and 11

Teacher
Joan Young, First and Second Grades

School
St. Thomas Aquinas School
Waterloo, Ontario, Canada

Concepts
Measurement, counting, estimating, place value, problem solving

Connections
Language arts, cooking

Materials
Ingredients for cookies, an oven, a large piece of brown paper

The children measured ingredients, mixed the cookie dough, and helped to bake the cookies. The cookies were placed on the brown paper to cool, in rows of 10 (unknown to the children). The children estimated how many cookies were baked and checked their estimates with counting by 1s, 2s, 5s, or 10s, whatever they felt comfortable with. After the cookies were removed and put in a cookie tin, the children used the grease marks left on the brown paper for counting, place value, and fractions activities.

Among the many skills the children practiced or learned while doing this project are measuring, estimating, problem solving, patterning, counting, skip counting, place value, and fractions. We also read *The Doorbell Rang* by Pat Hutchins to connect the math activities with literature.

Butterflies Chart

Pattern Book Experiments

▼

MATHEMATICS THEIR WAY
Chapter 12

Teacher
Diane H. Finucci, First Grade

School
Macomber Primary School
Westport, Massachusetts

Concepts
Pattern, counting, estimating, graphing

Connections
Science: insects

Materials
Chart paper, construction paper, scissors, tissue paper, markers, white glue

As part of a rain-forest unit, we raised six butterflies from caterpillars. After we set the butterflies free, I posed this problem: "I wonder how many wings our six butterflies had all together." Estimates ranged from twelve to ninety-four. We decided to make a chart to find the answer. As we placed our butterflies on the chart, we counted and recorded the number of wings. To end the lesson the children discussed the results and wrote an account of what we had done.

The children learned that when patterns were involved they could guess the next number in the series. One child even said, "I think we are counting by fours," and proceeded to explain his thoughts.

ngs ?

4

8

12

16

20

5 6 7 8 9

16 17 18 19 20 21

4

8

12

16

20

Jupiter

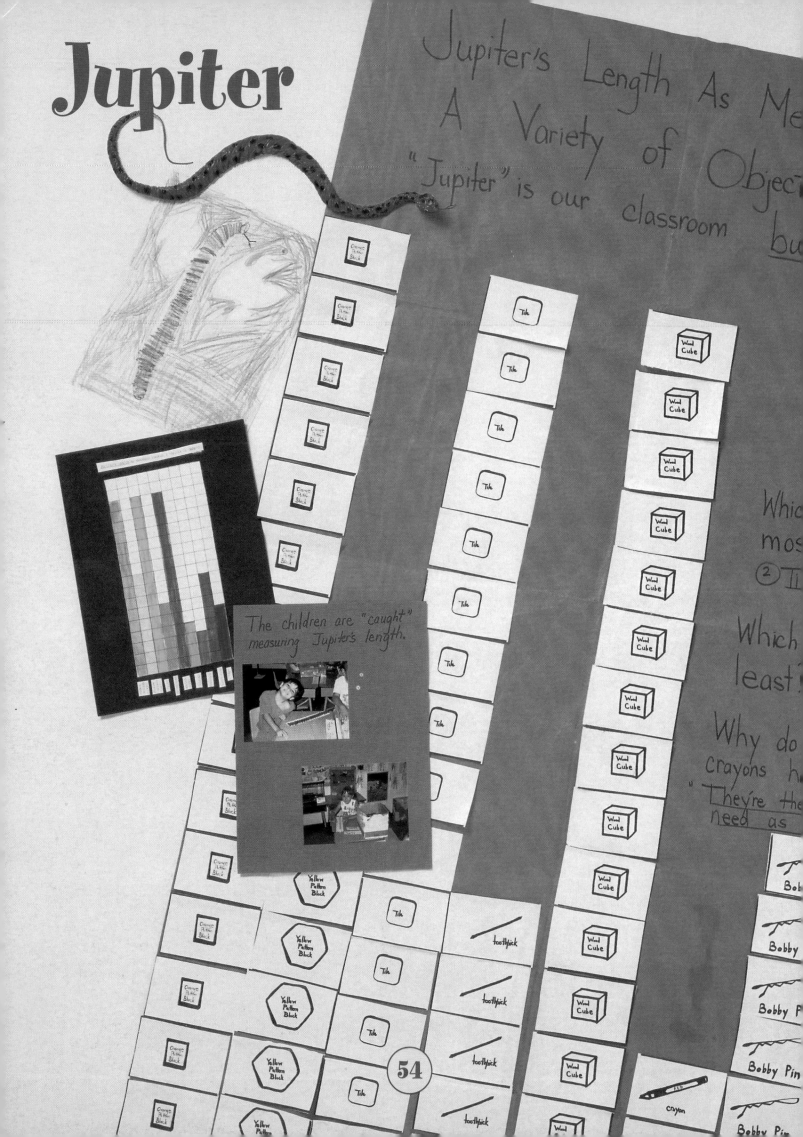

Jupiter's Length As Me
A Variety of Object
"Jupiter" is our classroom
bu

The children are "caught" measuring Jupiter's length.

Which
mos
② T

Which
least

Why do
crayons h
"They're the
need as

54

Patterns and Graphing

▼

MATHEMATICS THEIR WAY
Chapters 2, 6, and 10

Teacher
Janiece Ward, First Grade

School
Deanna Davenport School
El Paso, Texas

Concepts
Patterns, graphing, measuring

Connections
Science

Materials
A bull snake, various items for use for nonstandard measuring, chart paper, drawing paper

For an innovative and fun mathematics adventure, buy a bull snake for your classroom. The learning possibilities are limitless!

We had been studying patterns. When our newcomer arrived and was named Jupiter by the children, they immediately noticed the A-B pattern on his skin. Each child drew a picture of his dark brown, light brown pattern and we made a book of the drawings.

We extended the A-B pattern through multiple creative rhythmic patterns such as clap, snap, clap, snap; Unifix cube patterns; original junk box patterns; and verbalization of patterns that we saw in the classroom.

Each child was given a strip of paper the same length as Jupiter and was asked to "journey around the room" measuring its length with a variety of objects (pattern blocks, Unifix cubes, cotton swabs, crayons, markers, toothpicks, bobby pins, tiles, and an assortment of other junk box objects). We made a graph with the data that the children gathered. A child noted that three of the measuring materials (wood cubes, orange pattern blocks, and tiles) had the same amount and announced, "They must all be the same size!"

Jupiter and the discoveries that he helps children with have become a popular journal entry for the children. He has pulled the curriculum together in a very special way!

Whatimals

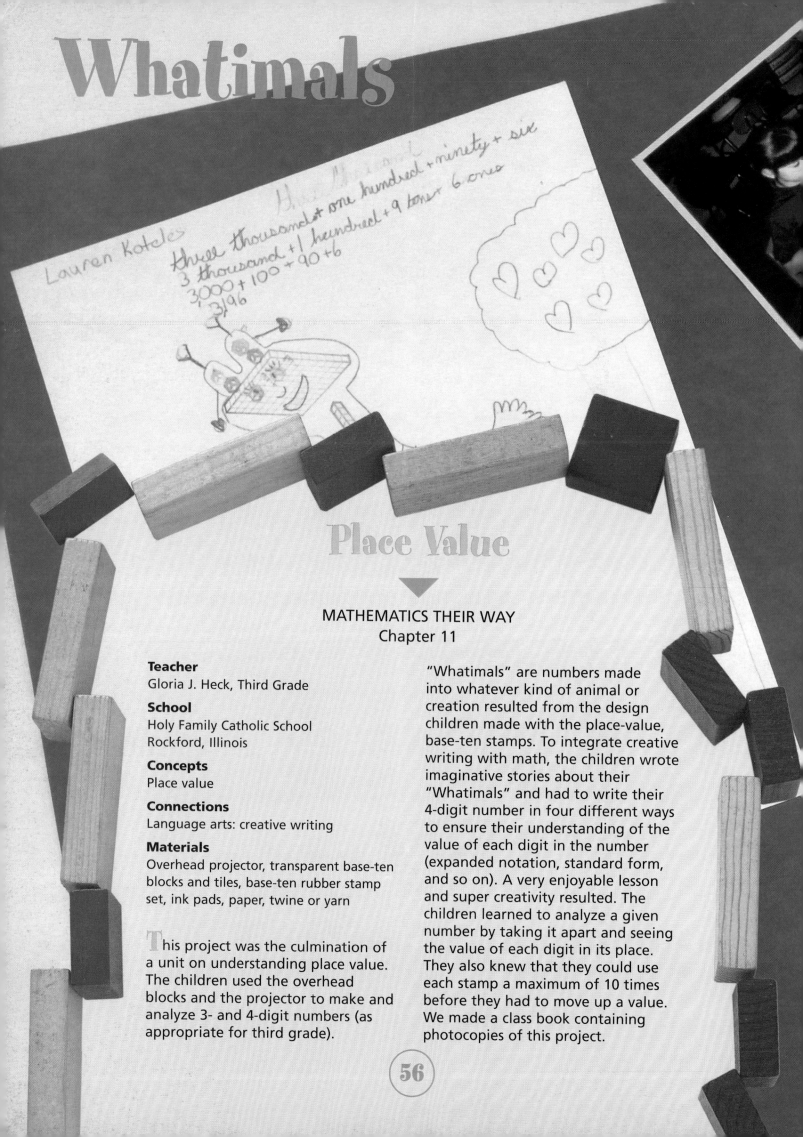

Lauren Kotcles

Three thousand + one hundred + ninety + six

3 thousand + 1 hundred + 9 tens + 6 ones

3000 + 100 + 90 + 6

3,196

Place Value

▼

MATHEMATICS THEIR WAY
Chapter 11

Teacher
Gloria J. Heck, Third Grade

School
Holy Family Catholic School
Rockford, Illinois

Concepts
Place value

Connections
Language arts: creative writing

Materials
Overhead projector, transparent base-ten blocks and tiles, base-ten rubber stamp set, ink pads, paper, twine or yarn

This project was the culmination of a unit on understanding place value. The children used the overhead blocks and the projector to make and analyze 3- and 4-digit numbers (as appropriate for third grade).

"Whatimals" are numbers made into whatever kind of animal or creation resulted from the design children made with the place-value, base-ten stamps. To integrate creative writing with math, the children wrote imaginative stories about their "Whatimals" and had to write their 4-digit number in four different ways to ensure their understanding of the value of each digit in the number (expanded notation, standard form, and so on). A very enjoyable lesson and super creativity resulted. The children learned to analyze a given number by taking it apart and seeing the value of each digit in its place. They also knew that they could use each stamp a maximum of 10 times before they had to move up a value. We made a class book containing photocopies of this project.

My thoughts about "Whatimals" are.... I learned how to write place value four different ways. I learned how to have fun doing math projects. It was the best

Lauren Koteles
Grade 3

October 13, 1993
Room 107

My Whatimal

My Whatimals name is "Heart" because she likes hearts. She lives in the heart forest. All week long except on weekends she grows heart trees! She will only eat things shaped like hearts! Shes 10,000 centreys old!!!! She has three legs, two arms, seven fingers, and skin like ours! She is twenty feet tall!!!! Her best friends are Boris, Betty "spaghetti", Rip, and Bimbum. Betty "spaghetti" just broke her leg a little while ago! Heart had to go over to her house for a long time! They were very, very, very happy! Heart likes reading, wrighting, and math!

Patterns at Home

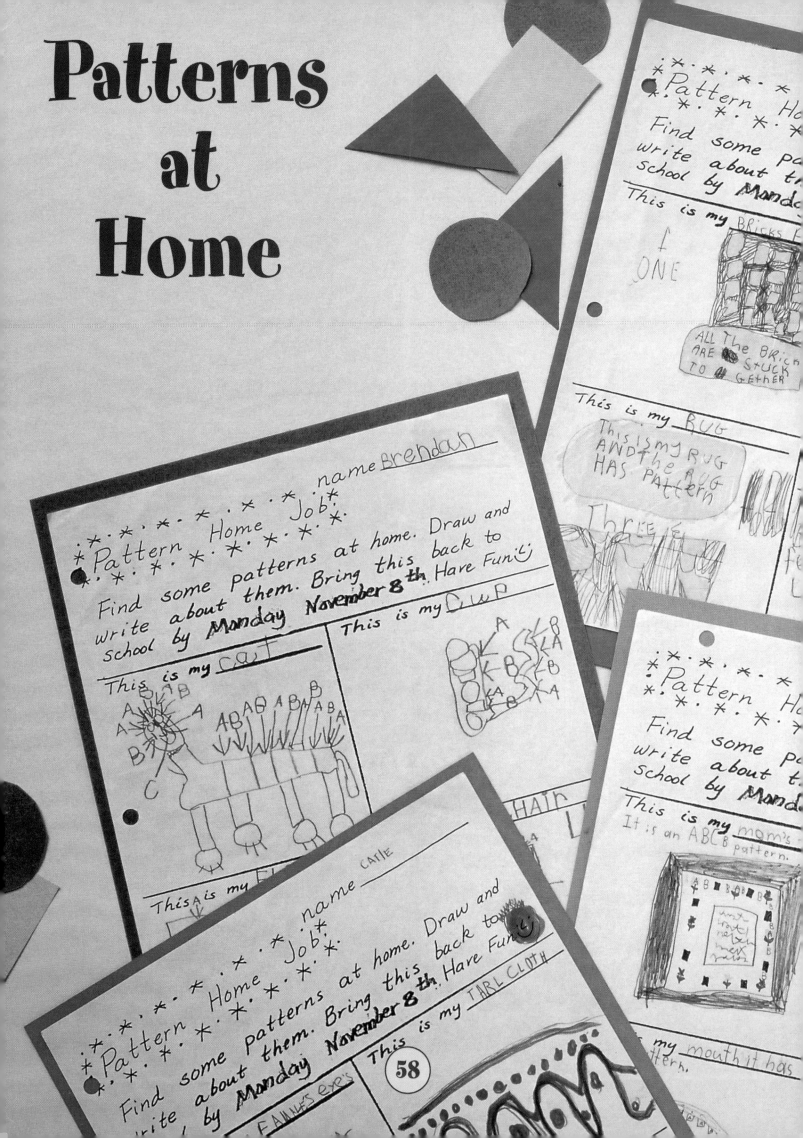

.*.*.*.*.*. name Brendan
.Pattern. Home. Job..
.*.*.*.*.*.*.*.*.*
Find some patterns at home. Draw and
write about them. Bring this back to
school by Monday November 8 th. Have Fun!

This is my CUP

This is my CAT

This is my _____

.*.*. name
.Pattern. Home. Job..
.*.*.*.*.*.*.*.*.*
Find some patterns at home. Draw and
write about them. Bring this back to
school by Monday November 8 th. Have Fun!

name CATIE

This is my TABL CLOTH

FAMILIES eye's

58

.*.*.*.*.* Pattern Ho
.*.*.*.*.*
Find some pa
write about t
school by Monda
This is my BRICKS

I ONE

ALL The Brick
ARE STUCK
TO GETHER

This is my RUG

This is my RUG
AND the RUG
HAS PATTERN

.*.*.*.*.
*.Pattern. H
.*.*.*.*
Find some p
write about t
school by Mond
This is my mom's
It is an ABCB pattern.

my mouth it has

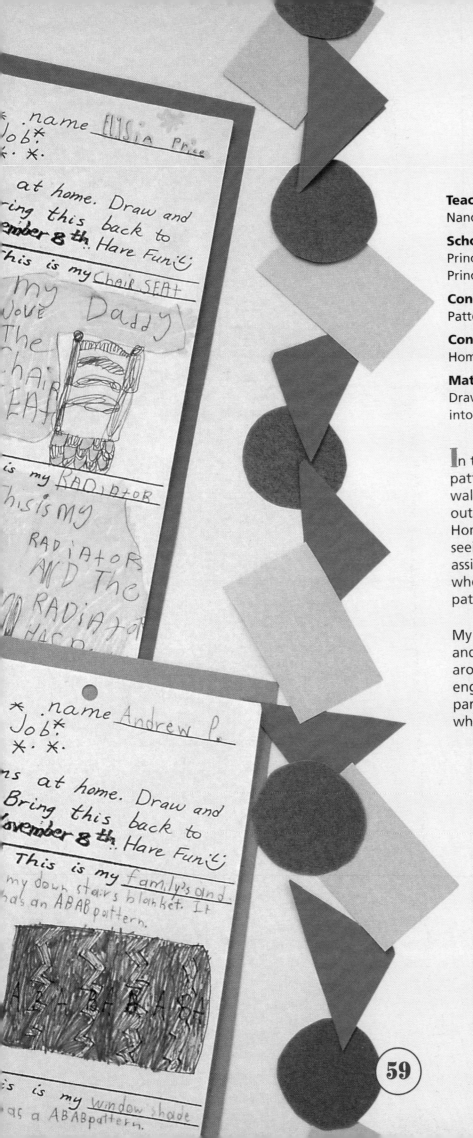

Patterns

MATHEMATICS THEIR WAY
Chapter 2

Teacher
Nancy Appel Boothby, First and Second Grades

School
Princeton Friends School
Princeton, New Jersey

Concepts
Patterns

Connections
Home-school, art

Materials
Drawing paper, twine or yarn for binding pages into a book

In the initial stages of our work with patterns, after we had gone on a "pattern walk," around school (in the classroom and outdoors), I used a worksheet for a Pattern Home Job for homework. I was interested in seeing who completed and returned the assignment, who worked independently, who with parents, and how elaborate the patterns and recordings were.

My students became increasingly enthusiastic and aware of patterns found in the world around them. They were much more engaged with our classroom work. Their parents also became more involved with what we were doing in the classroom.

Place Value

MATHEMATICS THEIR WAY
Chapters 11

Teacher
Cynthia K. Daniels, Kindergarten

School
Moon Mountain Elementary School
Phoenix, Arizona

Concepts
Estimating, measuring

Connections
Science: insects

Materials
Paper, crayons, scissors, glue

The children made and flew ladybug airplanes. To record their flights on math "flight sheets" they could use whatever manipulatives they wanted to measure each ladybug's flight. They learned that no two ladybugs flew the same. Some children offered explanations for the differences in flights: too much glue, not cut correctly, too windy, too heavy from crayons.

The children loved this culminating activity on insects!

The Flight of M

My ladybug will fly

My ladybug flew ____

I flew my ladybug ____

Ladybug Airplanes

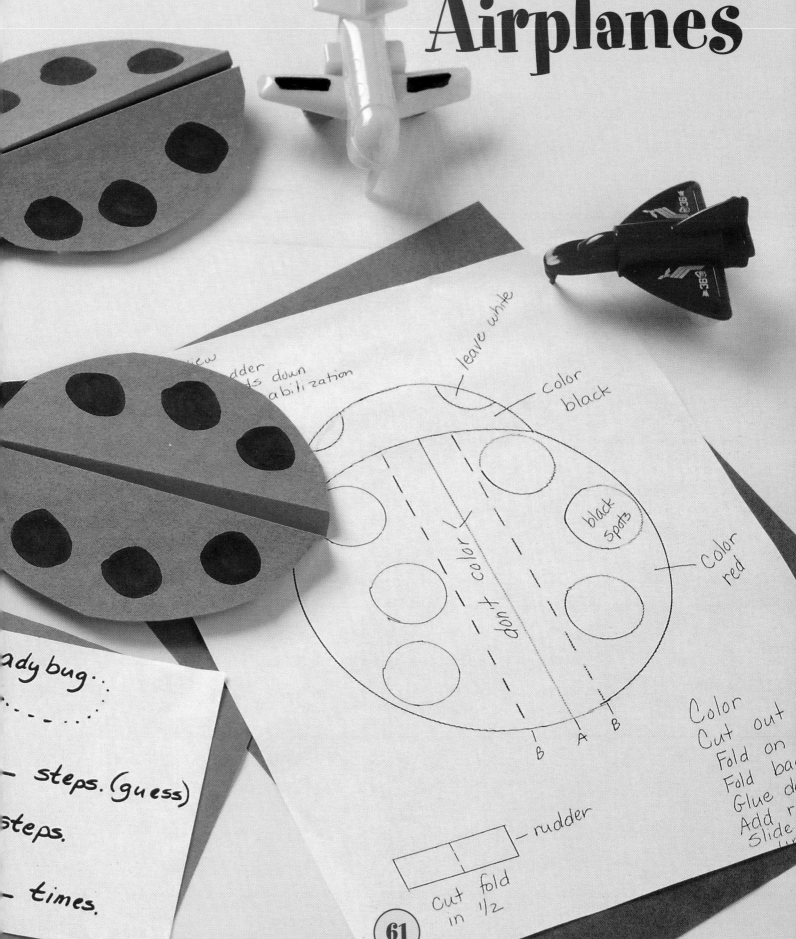

Labels on the diagram:
- view
- dder
- ds down
- abilization
- leave white
- color black
- don't color
- black spots
- Color red
- B   A   B
- Color
- Cut out
- Fold on
- Fold bac
- Glue do
- Add r
- Slide

- rudder
- Cut fold in ½

ady bug...
- steps. (guess)
- steps.
- times.

Pop-Up Shape Book

Rectangles have 2 sides that are short, 2 sides that are long. We see them as we walk along.

Circles Sorted By

Patterns

▼

MATHEMATICS THEIR WAY
Chapters 1, 2, and 10

Teacher
Joan Gresens, First Grade

School
St. Paul Lutheran School
Hazel Crest, Illinois

Concepts
Identifying geometric shapes

Connections
Language arts: creative writing

Materials
Old catalogs and magazines, scissors, construction paper, markers, pencils, large teacher-made pop-up books

This project could be a conclusion to many "shape hunt" activities. As they cut out and pasted shapes into the pop-up books, the children learned to identify geometric shapes. This activity particularly helped those first-graders who had difficulty transferring from hands-on to symbolic in pictures. We included a story-writing activity with the project, and all of the children who could wrote their own stories.

Graphing

▼

MATHEMATICS THEIR WAY
Chapter 6

Teacher
Lynda Baddour, First Grade

School
Durham Academy
Durham, North Carolina

Concepts
Estimating, measuring, fractions, counting

Connections
Language arts, science

Materials
Watermelon, large box, scale, yarn, yardstick, paper plates and cups, waxed paper, crayons or markers, glue, overhead graph paper, Watermelon Math books for students

A watermelon provided a full week of motivating mathematics for first graders. We began the week with Twenty Questions for the children to identify the contents of the large box covered with question marks. After discovering it was a watermelon, the children colored the covers of their Watermelon Math books. On the second day, we estimated the weight of the watermelon. To help estimate, the children used a five-pound bag of sugar to compare with the watermelon. After all the estimates were made, we discussed the answers, weighed the watermelon, and recorded the results in the Watermelon Math books.

Day Three involved estimating and then measuring the circumference with lengths of yarn. We graphed the results in three categories: *too short*, *just right*, and *too long*. Again results were recorded. On the fourth day, cutting up the watermelon for a treat led to a class discussion of fractions. Before eating their slices of watermelon, the children estimated how many seeds were in their slices, and then collected the seeds in paper cups as they ate the watermelon.

On Day Five, we counted the seeds, compared the results with the estimates, and graphed the results on an overhead graph. The week of Watermelon Math helped everyone learn that math is fun.

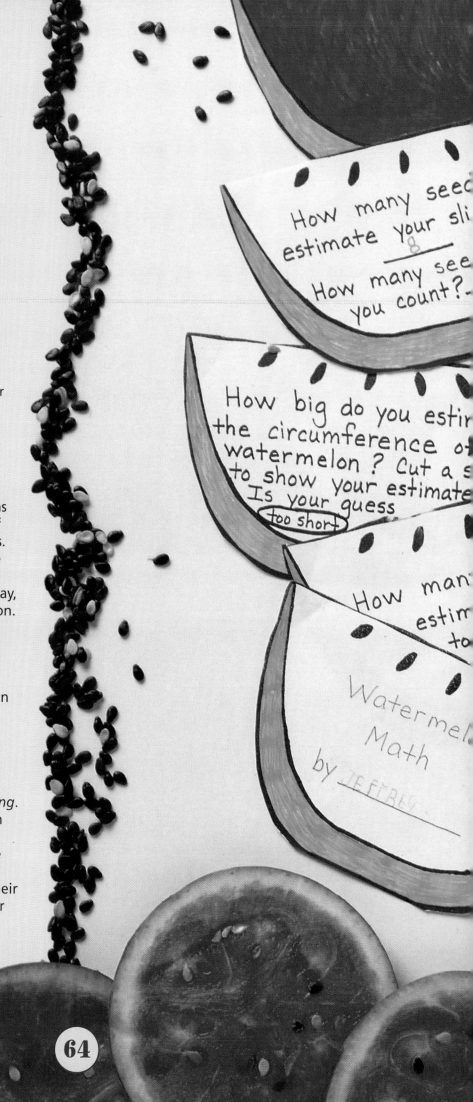

Watermelon Math

you
have?

ands do
our water-
gh?
weight [5]

We had __321__ Seeds
in our watemelon!

12
11
10
9
8
students 7
6
5
4
3
2
1

0-5 6-10 11-15 16-20 21-25 26-30 31-35 36-40 41-44

seeds

Class Results

name R

TEACHER INDEX